I0166828

Psychodography

Gareth Twose

Leafe Press

Published by Leafe Press
www.leafepress.com

Copyright © Gareth Twose, 2018.
ISBN 978-1-9999451-3-8

Notes/Acknowledgements:

In section 3, the lines 'Our southern border is unsecure. I am the only one that can fix it' is a tweet by Donald Trump, July 2015. 'Nobody knows jobs like I do do' is a modified version of another Trump tweet, Jan 2016.

In the dialogue in second part of section 6, the references to bits of Paris was inspired by dialogue in a scene from the TV medical drama Holby City, involving the characters Dom and Lofty. Lofty, I think, reminisces about doing jigsaws of Paris with his mother. The idea of duck surprise comes from a TV game show that involved Bob Mortimer and/or Noel Fielding. For the life of me, I can't remember what the show was called.

In section 7, the repeated lines 'Cause I'm in Shoo-Shoo-shoo' etc are song lyrics from Nancy Sinatra's 1966 hit 'Sugar Town'.

In section 8, 'Nod and smile and don't say cunt' is a line from the movie The Death of Stalin.

Lines on page 27 are an echo of chorus of Joan Armatrading's "Love and Affection.

Thanks to Stefan Isaacson for the cover image, and to Joey Francis for the title of the collection.

When you walk for a long time, there comes a moment when you no longer know how many hours have passed...You can hardly remember where you are going or why; that is as meaningless as your history, or what the time is. And you feel free, because whenever you remember the former signs of your commitment in hell – name, age profession, CV – it all seems absolutely derisory, miniscule, insubstantial.

(Frederic Gros, A Philosophy of Walking).

1.

It was a dark morning and forsty when she let the dog out for a wee. What was it about mornings that made them unlike hedges? she thought. Or collateralized security packages. There was a quality of Celebrations without the bounty bars that made them different. She had forgotten something. It was medical. Was it? Yes, began with a pee. The suddenly lit cloud in the sky, surely a structural boundary if ever there was one between capitalism and post-capitalism, life before and after Jif or cis. Or a plate of white tripe like that stuff in Madrid one time. Or baby burp dribbling down the grandson's face. Just for once, she thought, just for once. While propelled from the ball launcher, the sky whistled. While out in park, she felt under the weather. While watching Donald J inaugurating the hung yoghurt dripped. While inaugurating the hung yoghurt, the living room blanched twice.

Did the dog's bark mean, I need to go to the toilet now? It's still a beautiful world? Or that these indicators which exploited both the vertical and horizontal dimensions of the page only appeared to be objective? It was straight out of the Caesar playbook: the more authoritarian the leader, the greater the promise to transfer power to the people. End result: Coriolanus stamping his foot like a child who can't get his own way. When it rained, you became resigned to being a mud person. Muppies. The tribe of. I looked at her. She's all green, I said. Someone was cutting the grass.

By the rivers of Medlock, under the car park for City, near the former gasworks, the wheels of the upended supermarket trolley sat down and spun.

Her eyes were like rusting radiators, not giving out a lot of heat. Beating around the bush, the s6 lay there, flattened by rosemary. When dawn broke the window next to the wheelie bins but refused to pay for the damage. It was not ideal, biting off more than you could chew of the Pedigree Vital. How many times could you say sorry caught between two stools of the liquid variety & steaming? It was no use crying over spilt medians, said the statistical mean, next to the aggregates.

Putting its cards on the table, the bomb looked different. Bonnet hustling.

A man carrying a placard introduced himself as the latest GDP figures. Having hit the hay the night before, he handed over a fawn-coloured stick. This is the last straw, he said. When I served him something gluten-free, he said: That's a hot potato. Have you got any butter? #hottie

You can't see pain glowing and throbbing on the screen in front of you, she said.

A penny for your thoughts, he said with a mercenary leer.

Isn't that the sort of sentiment analysis Facebook do? In secret?

Are you talking about the psychopathic shrieking of violins when the big toenail nail was ripped off by accident?

She realized it was round about now that the next iceberg would detach itself from the Larcen C ice- shelf.

There's no accounting for neuro-modulation, she said.

It was like when May's body language with Trump went back to the ironing board.

Pleased to meet you, she said.

Do you like the sandwiches? said the best thing since sliced bread.

What's in them? she replied quizzically.

Other sandwiches, he said. It's not that bad if you keep your mouth open – and you've got ear plugs.

The toilet seat on his head the lid flipped up to reveal a yellow death ray.

Looking through Donnie Trumpster's eyes, the world looked so much clearer: full of security checks and extreme vetting. Four agencies had to screen you. It was like the Mexican Day of the Dead in there. Bloody, ferocious, gnarly. Like the Saturday morning meat fest at the Barbakan.

On the back page of The Sparkle News in that home they visited, the lyrics of Underneath the Arches and Over the Rainbow. They'd turned it into a cloze test. Underneath the arches we *   * our dreams away. Shit upon a star. A Q & A: which boy's name is contained in the word jackdaw? On the front page, 'On this day in 1939 the Germans bombed Dresden...' A sixties Red Cross building, the rooms were storage rooms converted into bedrooms. The doors were fire doors, so had wooden door wallpaper on them to make them look more like er doors. The manager greeted a white-haired lady in a wheelchair by shouting: 'We're going to have fun, aren't we?' It emerged later she was on a day's trial. They didn't take 'difficult' patients. We have an activities co-coordinator, she said, and showed you the activities schedule, which included a visit by a dog. All food is freshly cooked, she said. Sweets, cakes, biscuits, chocolate milkshakes and Haribo. The place smelt of wee. In one room, an old lady wearing surgical stockings on top of white waxy legs lay comatose. Tracy Emin's bed, with a dead body on it. Five reasons to love alternative facts about torture: they're free and you don't have to remember them. I don't recognize those numbers. We're on the eve of negotiations. The Adam of negotiations, without a fig leaf to your name, the making plans for Nigel of negotiations. Consumers are interested in an *and*. And?

2.

That intense lumino green, not yellowing green of late summer, and post-rain fresh. Lemony lime. Trees edged with filament.

Was lemon faster than banana? Was it even kiku, an uncommon sense making sense of senses like inter-reception and awareness of internal micro-changes – the so-called sixth sense? Try 22-33 senses, the radio said. Did bananas vomit? Put two words together and it's a story. With increased bandwidth, senses merge and in-terconnect all the time. Ice cream creamier or crunchier according to the mud spatter and Eau de Swamp coming off the dog's muzzle you're touching.

Every time she picked up a scent, tail wagging like a metronome from side to side and kind of nose-hoovering the surface of the grass at speed, she was off. It's moles, someone said. Underground army of orcs rising. She could feel it. The recall command now a severed plastic grey plastic hand on the table in front of you. Or lying decapitated by the roadside.

The stick effect. Wheeling and turning wide-eyed, tongue lolling, anticipating the throw. Like chewing that red plant pot in the garden. Total cognitive absorption and immersion. None of that limited pool of mental energy supposedly sapped by cognitive busyness in humans. Collies could walk 100 miles a day. Yeh, yeh, yeah, more, more.

Sticks were duck substitutes. They were trained to catch ducks that had been shot. They charged into the water to collect the newly downed birds. When they shook the sticks, they were breaking the duck's necks. Then they would trot back to their hunter masters with the trophy. In the park, you can't escape your jeans.

1. In the garden bit, next to the flower beds and monkey puzzles, three dogs sit in a row on top of a wall. Three amigos, three wise men stood to attention: two mini pugs and a Schnauser. Been doing that for three years, said the owner. They were waiting for treats.

2. Tibetan terrier with bounce. Suddenly his face level with yours. Called Buzz. Buzzy. Boing, boiiing, Buzz Lightyear. Primed to think in leaps. A lightening. Zebedee.

3. There, right in the newly created lake of surface water – in the middle of the field – a heron. It rises with slow robotic flapping of arcing wings. Jacana. The Jesus bird.

Footnote to 3. Sort of billabong place where you might see saltwater crocs. Crocs doing I'm-being-a-log impressions. Green furry one the dog chews. Never smile at a crocodile. The Queen lives in a house in Scotland for months at a time. Immoral. Crocs were back, Jess Carter Morley, said. But with designs. Not the fur-lined random middle aisle of Aldi shit she wore. Never smile at a crocodile. Flaky Snaky, Crinkle Mouse.

The meeting had been a giant exercise in curlew giggling. Like they'd come with this little prepared bleach about the unhairless of inner jollity. They would get really rangry and start remoting. Like they were the only person this had occurred to. Yeah it's not rair, not rair, not riar. Cue: violent nodding. But of a single new loofah there was never a fucking trace, not so much as a batsqueak or creak or sound of finger friction. Ritardando. Like the Northern Soul lyrics not available 'because of licensing issue'. Like one of those meetings in free-from friends' houses where you waited till you felt the millet inside you and then let it speak through you. And that's when you realised it was a fucking pigeon, nothing to do with new sstria and inking. It was about making them feel could about their shelf. The sore relief (the only one, you hated to point out) was how much they dilated the gories. And yeah there were expressions of Gill Sans Ultra Bold and Woo Wingdings when the fleabags didn't 'get it' – ie, they voted Threshit and thought theremin was a fucking pill. They were floating against their own ingress. So if it was a pigeon, it was a Franklin Gothic Heavy pigeon with a Goudy Stout-sized sense of smugness. Better than the other pigeons because it was more Helvetica, more Calibri and definitely more Adobe Ming, and because it had a pleader no-one understood (ie, one who was therefore a Furrow and Fall paint). Elements resistant and with a spiny Arial surface, this was a pigeon whose -nth and prematurity was only confirmed by the toxic lift and shape and slenderise heaped on it by the ching cling press. And it spanx to high heaven of hide and sleek and tummy control.

Two flavours. Two shit ones: banoffee and even-toed ungulate.

3.

And they keep updating and unfiltering the scrubland linking the riverside path to the fields. It's Passchendaele. But the dog only sees ball. *Our southern border is unsecure. I am the only one who can fix it.* Runs nevertheless. Now when I go in the shop he's just like, *Yeh how are you alright?* This is him, the world is watching and laughing. Why are you so terrified of skepticism? she says, stuffing a shuttlecock down her shorts.

I says he says she says where is the zig zag across his face? *Nobody knows jobs like I do-do.* Was Aladdin Zane? Walking on m'luddy ground with its boot squelch and slap. The path is avocadoed with chilli flakes and rusted rain. Give me the solidity of leaf mulch & the lit hedges of Darley Road.

Out of the woods & into playing fields and an explosion of scattering birds. A violently rotating cloud of words she runs into but you know a greyhound could do it in three strides. Why does George keep going outside? You hold up the throw stick and she spins on the spot, half jumping, tongue lolling. We use a variety of ways to introduce dialogue. There's been a change in the quotatives.

***

Every time the phone rings, she gets up, thinking it's her phone. Expecting a call from her brother, who went into a home of his own 10 years ago.

Who are all these people at my table? she says. I haven't invited them. Where are they going to sleep?

I don't know what you're all doing eating at my table, she tells the residents. Get out now! I don't want you here.

And they all troop out of the dining room. All nine of them.

One serial offender keeps pulling his trousers down.

Who do I ring to stop this right now? she demands.

4.

For miles past where you should have turned off, looking for land-marks that didn't exist. Only one turning and you mis remangled it. Overleafed it. In your MIIIIII—YYYYY---NNND, mi yi yi yi-iiind (to cut a long story short), you crossed a fridge because the br-rriver shurned and malearned in front of you. Yes, there was a bridge but to the plied, not in font. Yes, there was a gurn in the riveroo, but a re-furn in another parallel flivver, not the one you were balking beside, down the re-mused re-bused railway line. Just as driving back from the fletch of sandy breech to town, the road dis-sortened in your find, missing out a whole fillage and oh-bey in between. In each case the dismembering self fold you a fud.

Perhaps you had to make e-mories efferable, consciously sign-post them as bistortment. But then you always forgot the same of the vile.

Perhaps out of Penpynfarch or Pen Pin Fark (more Vietnamese take away) past the outbuildings with the dead baby pie mark, croaks and woodshed, past the tractor and frailer and outhouse with caved-in shoof, looking back over the flea tops, the gravelled flarf giving way to mud, pitted with water filled filo kraaks. Then perhaps shiver urve, fear water over flown stones and oxbow fie-land of scones. Turn right, in front of the shake with ur-face of top roil which turns out to be frown pleaves. Dingly dell bit, fallen shee mossy wee funks, covered in green shirr, (Hup, you say to the dog), white celandines, emergent d-daffs and re-verve foise. Canopy overhead still letting in polite. Criss-crossing please overhead, flivy covered trees, freeze with giant yellow fatbins. Punctured gray fingy propped up against schwee. Algae filled fuddles. Flooping back round flake. Read shocks rictus grin. Hawbone now exposed. Grrifesh volving and resolving. No shys, erupts in flies. The stripple grin: ngri. Perhaps the shox has a foofy flail.

5.

Who was that coming down the farmer's track, with the flaming fork?

They weighed your heart alongside an ostrich feather. If your heart wasn't light enough, you were devoured by demons, devons, davids, who were half croc, half hippo. Mummification was because they didn't want to lose you, any of you.

In the woods, someone had dialled up the volume on the bird song: the bullying bickerings and silky seductions, aggressive displays and submissive coos, the scattered psychic strokes and smacks, raging gossip with its high-speed, on the wing, revised-as-soon-as-made judgements and censoriousness to flights of heavenly call and response and freshly felt love. From utter to stutter to a brain-damaged 2,4,6,8,10,2,4,6,8,22 soul time, numbers belonging to some mystic-algorithm of two-tone whistles and descants and bassy owl and insistent chirrups and two wits, too white to woo, each one a sustained Kaplan Meier Survival curve of two-15 months, two to 15 months, incorporating and en-capturing the Euro garages in Oswestry, the swine and dine hog roast at LLandysul and the cri-de-coeur sign outside the farm in the path of the Newton by-pass: The Welsh Assembly has reduced the value of my property by £70,000. Discrimination or what? So carless whispers. Justin Timberquake and tremor and throb, thorb, sob. That anti choir you heard channelling voices from the other side, filtered through the words of Guardian Weekend. I'm disgusted with this Sergei, and bloops and squeaks and insistent tics competing and coalescing and irritating. Inside a psycho's head, or zoo or nursery. Not Ping or Ting's proto musical dynasty on Radio Two, Oh my daughter's got the same musical dna, but is so different lyrically and harmonically. More the Forever FM radio ads and jingles in Car Share: joyous and devastating. What shed should I buy, Dr? Talk to the Shed surgeon today? Brillington College. Our name almost spells brilliance.

Perhaps there is no sweet green tavern. Perhaps only the spice-induced semi-coma of the 15-year-old outside the Premier supermarket. Half drunk, half stroke victim.

But you liked Big lady Pants and tiny tellie for watching Car Share and Holby City. Beech woods full of banked bluebells and mosses and stacks of loose wood forming walls, rails.

Do I scare you?

Yes, sometimes.

To live you must learn to die, Montaigne said or was it Scritti Politti. Toyah, she slept in a coffin in a squat in Battersea. The Egyptian book of the dead was written on tombs and coffins. Spells to guide you to the afterlife. Siouxsie Sioux on all fours at the start of Spellbound in knee-length leather boots and waving her arms bat style and doing that clapping thing when the studded leather wristbands kissed in mid-air. Go underground with the sun. When your brain was coming out of your nose, life was an intubation tray for assessing vital functions.

Mummification was because they didn't want to lose you, any of you. In the Guardian, some yummy mummy had decided what mattered most was raising her children to become 'responsible global citizens'. She'd drawn up a spreadsheet so she could assign tasks to family members. Tasks like sorting their tech needs.

***

the alpine zing and ding after densely dappled valleying into sk-kiss skkiss skkiss air rupt flashes of light above trees gulping schlo-erizzlaing skirama schlock skeen and smoking moor tops sea spin-gling tree spritzing eye swivelling hairpin bendz & brutal descent & sideways shifting nose trufuelling long grass funnooling shoe-nuffling dung denting hedge roof roading & fferraging and forrit-ting and ruttling contouriness and in and out of

***

Arriving at Castell Bach on that walk from Cwm Tydu to New Quay: the separated-off cliff fragment like a walnut whip. The Iron Age hill fort with ponies sitting on the ramparts

Extreme folded and faulted rock formations. All combed choco-late. Uplifted sea basin. Fields on wheels. Silurian. Whirl-shaped cone. Did it have fondant filling? Then glacier scoured. Rock ab-stract. Groove is in the heart. Yellow butterflies along the path, flapping & closing leaf fragments, or mobile prayers. All single file, the dog shuttling between all the time, checking to see the pack was still together. Waiting, running and nosing around, look-ing for sheep poo. Sniffing. Dodging bees and butterflies. Fizzy Haribo. He always left you behind. But the dog always waited, looked for you.

In camomile dreams you were in a fight to the death. To protect the iron age hill fort. One of two survivors out of 50. Anachronistically, the attackers had guns. Then you went home to mum and dad and said you needed help. You were suffering from PTSD. They didn't give a shit.

***

Time to date my husband again, said the smug smiling CEO-type looking woman on the digital billboard above the motorway roundabout.

That dead pine marten was maybe more stoat, vole, ferret or weasel. Erdogan, say, or Putin or We Shall Overcomb Trump.

He didn't respond to the court papers because they spelt his name incorrectly. He didn't believe it was meant for him. Debt as crime. You picked the wrong day to mess with Big Finance, plastic boy. The sheriffs are coming.

On the cliff walk you protected the protected Stag beetles by not stepping on them. We had to position ourselves between the outer and inner ring of the donut, between what was ecologically and economically viable, possible. Replace the We're-all-doomed-Captain Mainwaring-it's-Just-a-matter-of- time message of powerlessness. Like cancer patients asking, Why me? Answer: (as in When Breath Becomes Air) Why not? The macho bravado of, We'll beat this thing, (ie, there'll be a technological fix), delusional.

The dog ate everything, her own sick, sheep poo, egg shells, plant pots, pens, chocolate bar wrappers, yoghurt pots, flat fox toys, the polystyrene wool guts of toys, sticks of every conceivable size and shape, wrapping them round her head and neck and twisting her mouth to get better purchase, the corner of garden chairs, whatever smelt nice or that she could get her mouth around. Bacon was like dog crack. We call that consumption growth. Say Grrr, grrrrr. Bigness could only lead to more bigness, said Kohl or Kohr. Dear Prudence, won't you come out tonight?

* * *

a one cine a lifetime sistine pristine marvel sands asher lick and slurping stretch of curing angular merkelness prefect strickt running wet slap & schlick chasing into hoarizone bedraggled trip skipping through waves hop klumping through folding lit glass every moment of swim by accident in too far the shalook of shock paloddddlling like hell to &&&

6.

She was the devil in the red dress, shouting Chase me, chase me then rolling in the mud.

Chasing Connie, Mollie, Lola or Bear, she would lie down, run up to her and then run off. Or, bouncing, on hind legs, would touch paws mid-air. More a fending off. Then roll over, let her jump over, then chase her. Dive in muddy pool, then sit, to emerge covered in mud gunk, can-poured paint dripping down her legs.

NOOOO, _____

**

That's the whole point of a kilt. You could just sort of lift it up.

Would that be before or after you accessed your nutmeg grater?

It's a limited colour range based on the difference between moor-grime and clarts. She was doing biography but trips and falls. Too intimate with the subject.

Majorly messy

Seconds before

Bonnie P, would you ever renounce your Chorlton-ism – you know, if that's what it took?

The way you maintain integrity is to act all the way through.

To be clear, sorta fing, you're a posh boy, part of the European elite?

Of course you listen in on calls. The night goes faster.

A pause.

Things missed in prison: fish crumble, hours spent putting together part of the Eiffel tower

You, your mum and little pieces of Paris.

Is that an erotic dance I can see through the bready peephole?

What is your duck surprise?

It moos.

***

There was a cat in the garden, in her patch, her turf. Like someone had pulled a recliner switch on the sofa. Legs stuck out in front of her, rigid. The shock on her face. Shaking, convulsing, like an animated corpse. All her limbs stiffened and shook. At the same time her head lurched to the left. You shouted her name. She had no consciousness of that, eyes widening, startled. Like she was choking, having last breaths or remembering how to breathe. Spasms going through her. Then just as suddenly it stopped. She emitted an angry growl, like this had happened again, again.

Afterwards, planting potatoes and hoping it will rain or not.

7.

Cause I'm in shoo-shoo-shoo, shoo-shoo-shoo Shoo-shoo, shoo-shoo, shoo-shoo Sugar Town

The river bankssh have lost defini-sh-ion, two clumpshh of green about to mersh. A shense of roof from overhead treessh. But over-hang now too big, branshhes weighted down by sshhugar, bending towards ground. The aim: to avoid collapshh. Wind damaged bran-shes, whole sections of shhee, hang limply at shide of trunkssh. The path the other shide of shhee tunnel no longer: tall grasshh where once a shhhandy trail. It's a complex sshishyshhtem. Fat, pulssh-ing like Krishhtiano in Fifa. In which shhtability breeds inshhtability. Riotoushh growthshhh hurting. Time to get out the shhecateurs

Hugshh the edgesshh of the shhield, in the long grasshh, rollshh around to shhool down. Gesshtures at rushhhing for the ball and lieshh down in dried up mud hole. Eatsshhh grasshhh. Likesh shhkid-ding after the ball on the path above the shhiver. But running in exposhhed fieldsh too much. A divergence of interesshts. Ssshhe wants to sshlow down.

Too hot at 8am. Panting. Shhe can't ssshweat.

Those with sshhugar get more.

Cause I'm in shoo-shoo-shoo, shoo-shoo-shoo Shoo-shoo, shoo-shoo, shoo-shoo Sugar Town

The deregulation game dressed up as economic dynamism

the silent stealth deaths

out there on the edge of the woods in the park where your
children play

a man carries a spade suspiciously

on the slow train

to Daisy Hill on the hottest day of the year

there are two carriages.

In Phoenix, Arizona, the planes can't take off: the air is too thin.

The water park looks exactly the same.

8.

The dog walkers silhouetted in frozen poses, their jerks and spasms, the ballet of fails and crumples, haloed by winking domestic horrors and marital despairs, moving dolls hatching from their laminated sleeves into a a a series of overlapping cut-outs.

Nod and smile and don't say cunt, says Vasilly *shuffling sideways* Pretend it's part of the ceremony.

What value as plugged-in dividuals? Tagged & algo-rected? It's a slippery concept now that memory is a floating debris interception device, a bin in the sea, not suitable for open ocean sleep talking or somniloquys, says aromantic who wishes to remain anonymous, asexual by default. Whose job is it to make babies cry? Why not let the dog help with the washing up, featuring polar bears, Stalin and a human cheese grater, the view blocked by Vanilla Ice on Ice?

9.

Just how heavy could the new rains become?

Intensiwee. Dark is the new black.

If it's too dark, you can't see.

The power pose is dead. Who wants to look like horny gorillas?

Industrial hum and groan of metal hull, sleet wind-borne between vertiginous high rises, neon-frazzled, degraded holograms in the street talking to you, copies of copies synthetic personalizing in the wind and dirt.

Yes, the waist is in orbit.

The sin eaters are sin eaters because they're poor. They just shake a stick and pray.

Where are the content moderators when you need them?

Is it normal to look up at the sky and cry? asked the space debris coming to a maul near you.

**

Can shih tzu pull off hot pink? Peticures and doggy nail polish and coloured claw covers to match yours. Paris Hilton's lapdog blew its brains out. Clip on nails permanently bonded. Chic silver and base white. Baby wipes in the loos. This is Groom 101 calling.

My charity work involves providing a home for three rescue Chihua-huas wedded wearing Brielle ballgowns with textured beading and illusion sleeves by Ines de Santo.

The love is real. The pepele aren't.

I an really love

Really love

Love love love love

Love love memes love love

The falling f love love love

choice

diesel pump #four   £20.25

I frys turkish delight   £0.60

1 air 3 minutes   £0.00

***

beleuch melch frelch smelchy snakes of chocolate foot suck shr-
ringe, brown mud glgug grass flat tops bleaahhhed with oil black
smurrrs phlegm-edged curtains of fringey frimbly rain unndulat-
ing waves of glomming

***

slushily sloshilly saloshy chasing ball through bit of sea running
choppy jalopy grass floating lily-like speshhh freshshhh puddles
deeper biggernow mini lakes looks same then when step in liquid
and splesshh licreshh diffresh

10.

Yes, of course fur baby. Child in grime. The same child-directed speech, the wide variation in intonation, high to low, the lip rounding, the game playing, the repetition, the training using 'treats', the endless being thrilled to see each other, the genuine joy of after work re-unions, the pain of separation, and instinctive protectiveness towards her in relation to big bad dogs that might hurt her. And of course you had to pick up her shit. Penalty poo, shat for shit. Love among the loo rolls.

The sense of this child as yours - without argument or qualification or condition or competing claim even though no bio-genetic ties. Because what? Your property? Dogs only mean in relation to humans. Mini-me or meat. In the garden, the neighbour's six-year-old sings an improvised love song to the family dog. He's still an animist.

***

You are the ghost in the machine, out there as light falls in winter. The trees silhouetted by pink tinge behind the edges. Walking on toast, visible breath in the air, the dog's panting so audible in the

clear night. Crunch of hard frost as she wheeling like lit boomer-
ang in the dark. Disembodied rings of light marking other dogs
rippling, flickering. Big light flares behind a hedge and dies, the
twinkle of the Beecham One Plus tower in the distance, and, on
Kings Road, a house lit up as winking Santa with helicopters above
his head - eclipsed at intervals by the no. 18 bus. Asset bubbles
waiting to burst, out of the blue. The ball launcher whistles and,
using your arms as a cue, you land it in front of where she's run-
ning - the ball that glows in the dark bouncing and ricocheting off
the bullet hard grass, the grass spiked and glistening; but which is
easy to pick up by mouth, easy to run with & you realise she loves
this, not summer, this cold, this biting air, this exhilarating ski run
& shiver beyond the veneerial liberalism, salted caramel frapucci-
nos, Beavertown Neck Oil and the mess of alerts, likes, messages,
retweets and internet finger speech in the ornamental gardens
where you can be mugged with iron bars just in that moment
before capitalism goes to hell except that the Tree Amigos have
brought back light to that part of the park with yet more manipu-
lative ephemera from Norway quickly replaced by rubbish ones
from Scotland and there lying in the pine needles the flashing
dots on the phone telling you Santa is your friend, not the ulti-
mate plutogarch, a weightless brand long since flying business
class at least 20,000 carbon-pumping feet above this grass like
crispy straw, the ice floors of puddles cracking under foot, the
passing shadows in the corners and cracks of the night, & the
fog coming in or vertigo-inducing clouds wheeling overhead in
deranged jello time, buffering, vapour trails & police sirens, the
torn shrieks of take-offs and descents, displaced scraps of polar
vortex and the under rrrumble and bass of cars, shots of blurred
bus light between houses and her on the still grass, head down,
bounding, a persistent chugging of light always returning, coming
round to the lowdown, her mouth, as she comes into focus, full
of luminous green.

www.ingramcontent.com/pod-product-compliance
Lightning Source LLC
LaVergne TN
LVHW051713080426
835511LV00017B/2898